MANSFIELD
PAST & PRESENT

A jam manufactory was started by George Pickard in 1885 in the former Congregational Chapel off Stockwell Gate. After his death in 1905 his two sons managed the business until 1931. The premises were demolished in 1973.

MANSFIELD
PAST & PRESENT

THE OLD MANSFIELD SOCIETY

WHSmith

First published in the United Kingdom in 2002 by
Sutton Publishing Limited exclusively for
WHSmith, Greenbridge Road, Swindon SN3 3LD

British Library Cataloguing in Publication Data
A catalogue record for this book is available from the British Library.

ISBN 0-7509-3163-9

Illustrations

Front endpaper: Market Square, *c.* 1900.
Back endpaper: Drawing of Mansfield Brewery, 1907.
Half title page: Borough of Mansfield Civic Regalia.
Title page: Co-operative Society building before 1961.

Typeset in 11/14pt Photina and produced by
Sutton Publishing Limited, Phoenix Mill,
Thrupp, Stroud, Gloucestershire GL5 2BU.
Printed and bound in England by
J.H. Haynes & Co. Ltd, Sparkford.

Stanton Mill on Bath Lane, 1951.

Contents

This scene is one that is never likely to be seen again in Mansfield. The recent closure of the Mansfield Brewery marks the end of the brewing of beer in the town. The company was founded in 1855. New premises were built on Littleworth in 1907, an illustration of which can be seen on the back endpaper. The date of this photograph is not known but it could have been taken before the 1950s.

Introduction

One evening in May 1900 my father, then a boy of four, was taken by his father from their Duke Street home to the Market Place. There they joined an excited, jubilant throng of people who had gathered to celebrate the relief of Mafeking, a town in distant South Africa besieged for seven months by the Boers and recently liberated. As if by magic, flags and bunting appeared, coloured lights burned in front of the Town Hall and the Excelsior Band played patriotic music before leading a procession to the home of the mayor, Councillor Chadburn. It is doubtful if many in that vast crowd had far to walk as Mansfield was still a compact town, its houses tightly packed around the market and the five roads that radiated out from it. There was some spread but it was limited and usually confined to large villa-like houses built for some of the more prosperous members of the community. Typical of these were the brothers George and Robert Alcock, both well-to-do hosiery manufacturers, the former living on Nottingham Road, the latter on Woodhouse Road. Although some of the newer houses were of stone, most were of brick. Green fields still surrounded the greater part of the town. Just as no one lived far from the Market Place, so no one lived far from the countryside. Walking was a popular pastime and Sunday afternoon was a time for a pleasant stroll amid the rural delights so close at hand.

The extent of the town has certainly changed during the past hundred years – and so has almost every other facet of its appearance and life. The population has more than trebled from 21,445 in 1901 to around 60,000 in 2001 and the necessary housing has increased accordingly. At first this was provided by private developers but they could not satisfy the ever-growing demand, especially in the years following the First World War. It was clear that more radical measures were necessary, and so the borough council attempted to ease the situation by providing a number of houses. It began modestly at the end of 1919 when work started on a small development off Baums Lane but progressed more ambitiously in the following year when the first roads were laid out on the future Bull Farm estate. By 1930 more than five hundred houses were in occupation there. Across the town another large estate was spreading over former agricultural land at Ravensdale. Although further plans were in hand, all building work, both council and private, ceased in 1939 on the outbreak of the Second World War.

So great was the demand for homes after the war that emergency measures had to be adopted and three hundred prefabricated houses were constructed. Although regarded as 'temporary' with an anticipated life of no more than twenty years, some of these houses, suitably modernised, are still in occupation. Work began on the vast Ladybrook estate in 1950 and, while homes were still rising there, land was acquired for the Bellamy Road estate. A total of 1,270 council houses were built between the end of the war and 1952.

The market has always been a busy place, overlooked by the centrally placed Bentinck Memorial.

In contrast, private development had provided only 284 dwellings. Bricks and mortar continued their outward march with the Oak Tree estate, private developments in the Berry Hill area and other smaller schemes about the town. By the end of the century Mansfield's houses ran up against those of the neighbouring communities of Sutton-in-Ashfield, Pleasley, Mansfield Woodhouse and Rainworth. Anyone contemplating a walk into the countryside now would have to cover several miles before leaving the urban scene.

The town's appearance is very different, too. Many of the photographs in this book illustrate this fact more eloquently than words can describe. Certainly, a good number of old buildings survive but all too often they are isolated examples and while this isn't always a bad thing it can be detrimental to the townscape if the replacements are poorly designed or built of unsympathetic materials. Happily, towards the end of the twentieth century more thought was given to the conservation of interesting buildings and to the appearance of new ones. White Lion Yard is a good example of this. This Church Street property consisting of an inn, shops and dwellings had clustered around a small courtyard for centuries. The oldest part dates back to at least 1584. Over recent years its condition had deteriorated to such an extent that it looked a prime target for the bulldozer. In the past this may well have been its fate but in these more enlightened times it has fared much better. The whole block has been carefully restored and now provides accommodation for a restaurant, two shops and storage facilities while three small caves, hewn from the indigenous sandstone, have been set out as a visitor centre. Now both townspeople and visitors can see how this part of old Mansfield has evolved through four centuries and discover who lived there and the work that they did.

With five main roads funnelling into a central market place, Mansfield can never have been an easy place to pass through. At the beginning of the twentieth century the horse still ruled the road though bicycles were becoming more popular. By 1903 no fewer than eighteen local men owned motor cars. Two years later trams added to the congestion, but they provided a cheap and convenient means of travel through the town and to the neighbouring villages. They lurched and rattled their way along the main streets until 1932 when they were superseded by buses. Since then road traffic has increased to such an extent that its management has become one of the town's major problems. One-way systems, limited on-street parking, pedestrianisation: all have been tried but found wanting in adapting the town's historic street plan to the needs of present-day traffic. It was obvious that something more drastic was called for and this was introduced in the last decade of the century when the inner ring road, long in construction, was completed. This may have alleviated the situation to a certain extent although it has not met with universal favour and has brought its own problems to perplex the local authorities.

In 1900 it was said that more trains used Mansfield's Midland Railway station than St Pancras in London. Whether this was so or not has not been proved, but certainly

The railway station on Great Central Road.

Precision engineers working on a 'memory drum' at Boneham & Turners in 1965.

Mansfield was a busy railway centre for both passenger and freight traffic, even though it didn't stand on a main line.

After the Great Central Railway opened its station in the town in 1917 local people could, for a short time, travel to London without changing trains. Gradually, however, services were withdrawn over the years and in 1964 all passenger trains ceased and the station was closed. And so it remained until 1995 when, renamed the Robin Hood Line, passenger trains began again to run to Nottingham and later to Worksop. Although quite heavily used, it is still only a branch line, its trains not often connecting conveniently with main line services.

Although vestiges of its agricultural past remained and it was still regarded as a market town, Mansfield in 1900 was essentially an industrial centre. Long looked upon as its staple industry, framework knitting may have been in decline but textile mills lined the banks of the River Maun and foundries, engineering works, maltings, a brewery and sundry other factories were dotted about the town. As if waving farewell to the town's agricultural past, several windmills still turned their sails to face the prevailing wind. They may have been survivors of the past but signs of the future were also apparent. Coal mines had been drawing closer to Mansfield from the west and north but in the opening decade of the twentieth century colliery headstocks could be seen from the town itself. In 1902 Sherwood colliery was sunk just within Mansfield Woodhouse, to be followed two

Mansfield's numerous foundries gave employment to many men and boys. Only one remains now.

years later by Crown Farm colliery at Forest Town. Work for many townspeople was in the factory, mill, workshop or down the mine. Although the hours were long, the labour often grindingly hard, the safety standards sometimes lax and the pay poor, there was a feeling of permanence in such employment. Work, however onerous, even unpleasant, would always be there.

How different the situation is a hundred years later. Both coal mines have closed, their only visible remains are the grassed-over waste tops, a few tubs in public parks and occasional winding wheels marking the entrance to the former collieries. Other industries, long regarded as fundamental to the town's economy, have fared no better. Textile and hosiery mills have closed, the premises of the last working maltings now houses a night-club and the Mansfield Brewery is currently up for sale. But the Sherwood Foundry is still in business; Barringer, Wallis & Manners, later the Metal Box Company and now Carnaud Metalbox Speciality packaging, continues in production; and Boneham & Turner, precision engineers, attracts business throughout the land. There are other survivors, of course, but the closure of the more traditional and more labour-intensive industries has created problems of unemployment that are proving difficult to overcome. Attempts are constantly being made to attract new industries to the town and, although some success has been achieved, too many townspeople are still without work.

In the older photographs of street scenes, most of the shops shown were privately owned, the more fashionable occupying prominent sites around and close to the market place. Apart from the emporium and the branches of the Mansfield Co-operative Society, it is doubtful if there were more than a handful of shops of outside ownership in the town. The incursion of the multiple stores was a feature of the first half of the century but as it was a gradual process it was largely seen as a welcome supplement rather than a serious challenge to the local shops. This was not so with the coming of supermarkets and megastores in the second half of the century. They have transformed the pattern of shopping, usually vacating the town centre and building their massive retail centres on the outskirts where adjacent parking space is available and provides an additional incentive to custom. Of course, this has affected the traditional shopping area. Many shops, some of fond memory, have closed. There are too many vacant premises although the town centre is still a lively, even bustling place, especially on market days, and judicious shoppers can usually satisfy most of their wants there.

The theme of change during the twentieth century can be taken further. In the early years churches and chapels sought to expand their witness, new places of worship were built and congregations were, on the whole, large. Sadly the passing years have wrought a dramatic change. Some of the churches that opened in such optimism and joy have now closed, congregations in others are generally smaller, though there are exceptions, and some are finding it a struggle to continue. Mansfield's schools have been in the mixing bowl on more than one occasion during the past century. In 1900 there were grammar and elementary schools plus some private establishments. For a short time Mansfield became a local authority responsible for its own schools and appointing its own director of education. Under this system, in the inter-war years, fine modern schools were built at High Oakham and Ravensdale, the former becoming widely famed because of the excellence of its choir. The Education Act of 1944 brought Mansfield under the control of the Nottinghamshire Education Committee and introduced the secondary modern school to the town. Subsequent reorganisations have closed the grammar schools, brought in comprehensives, experimented with middle schools and, finally, adopted an orthodox two-tier system of education. For the sake of the children and their teachers it is to be hoped that a period of greater stability will now prevail.

In a century of widespread change, it is interesting to note one instance of a reversal to what had previously pertained. Mansfield had only been a chartered borough for nine years in 1900 and proudly looked to its mayor as its chief citizen. This position was swept away in the local government reforms of the 1970s. However, the people of Mansfield have recently voted to restore the office of mayor. The mayor will be elected and will have very different responsibilities from those who bore the title in the past. It is to be hoped that this move will be to the good of the town, that the years ahead will be a time of economic progress and of beneficial environmental development, and that Mansfield will be a place where people are happy to live.

Michael Jackson
August 2002

Trade & Commerce

The Co-op Society store on Stockwell Gate, before 1961. The needs of small-town Mansfield used to be met by local businesses. The introduction of the Co-op store saw the arrival of new and larger firms to the town. They required new premises, which helped in the redevelopment of the town centre. Many built on a grand scale, especially the new banks which came to the town. This process continues today, sometimes to the detriment of the town, as national and multinational stores establish themselves away from the town centre in out-of-town retail parks.

Mansfield Co-operative Society was formed in 1864, selling food and household necessities from a shop rented from the landlord of the adjacent Masons Arms public house. The opening hours were limited to evenings only, because the committee members who served in the shop were at their own work during the day. The Society flourished, despite the hostility shown by other shopkeepers. In 1866 larger premises were taken on Stockwell Gate and a flour mill and bakery were built on Queen Street. A serious fire here in 1882 necessitated a rebuilding. Another fire in October 1918, which began in the basement café of the Stockwell Gate premises, seriously damaged both building and stock. Trading continued from branches in the town until the rebuilding was completed in 1922. A prominent clock tower dominated the premises and a system of overhead wires and cylinders transported cash from counters to a central office. Further extensions in 1935 and 1959 and the removal of the clock tower in 1961 altered the store's appearance. When the Four Seasons Shopping Centre opened in 1976 a bridge connected the older building to new departments in the centre.

The Dividend was a vital source of extra money to the household budget of share-holders and could be as large as *2s 6d* in the pound. This is the 1938 'Divi' queue on Queen Street. Since then the lower part of the Co-op building has been modernised and this part of Queen Street pedestrianised. The bus is on the route to Sutton and Huthwaite.

Small temporary shop units on the upper part of Stockwell Gate in the 1960s. They comprised a newsagent, hairdresser and dry cleaners. They were demolished at the same time as the Four Seasons development was being built to make way for a supermarket.

The standard of hygiene in Mr Oakland's butcher's shop was no better and no worse than in other similar establishments in the town. Most were open to the elements and subject to the attention of passing flies, dogs and children's fingers. This building stood where the corner of Marks & Spencer's is now. The alleyway between the two buildings was known as Thompsons Alley; it was one of many that once ran between the buildings in the old town.

Crow & Leckenby's tea-room, opened in 1902, initially occupied only a small part of the building but after later expansion Leckenby's became a very popular high-class provision dealer. It remained in business into the 1960s, and is still affectionately remembered, especially for the coffee aroma that exuded from the store. The dragons that crowned the building have mysteriously disappeared.

Boots the Chemists had premises on Leeming Street before it moved into the Four Seasons Shopping Centre. Since then the building has accommodated a number of different traders.

Macfisheries was one of the earliest supermarkets in the town, with a fish shop lower down on Leeming Street. The site has since been occupied by many firms and has recently undergone extensive refurbishment to become a wine lodge.

Main Streets &
Back Streets

The Lurchills ran between Woodhouse Road and Rosemary Street and was the way for vagrants to avoid the town centre on their way to the workhouse.

Aerial view of the
town centre with the
Market, the Co-op
and the West Gate
prominent, 1950.

Slightly off-centre is a cruck building dating from the medieval period. Its main structure was made up of oak timbers roughly in the form of an inverted V. Such buildings are comparatively rare. In spite of efforts to retain the timbers they were eventually destroyed. The building had a chequered career as a blacksmiths, a general store, a café (Caunts), Ye Olde Refreshment House in the 1920s and finally Bayliss's newsagents. To the right of the cruck house is the entrance to the King's Head inn.

The view up Belvedere Street, 1936. Wards, the Little Stores, Chatterton's and the Tudor House have all gone. The pub, the Crown, is still there but is now called Hucksters.

The junction of Rosemary Street, Belvedere Street, Stockwell Gate and Sutton Road in 1956, before the present ring road and bus station were built. On the left is the Empire Cinema. The big building to the left of Rosemary Street was a Methodist (later Baptist) chapel. Tesco's superstore is on the site of the hoardings, and the imposing clock tower on the Co-op was dismantled in 1961.

These properties on Rosemary Street, between the Rosemary Schools and Goldsmith Street, were built as houses but converted into shops soon afterwards. Before the Rosemary Schools opened in 1900, the street was a narrow lane with fields on one side and only a few isolated houses. Extensive development then took place and all reminders of the agricultural past near the town centre disappeared. A doctor's surgery, Mill View, now occupies this site.

Most of the old buildings on the left-hand side of Stockwell Gate have retained their old frontages, apart from the Co-op. The ornate front of what was once the Blue Boar inn has been sympathetically restored by the building society that now occupies it.

Little has changed in this block of buildings on Stockwell Gate, as viewed from the side of the market in the early 1970s.

Lloyds Bank now occupies this building. The shops to the left of the entrance to Sadler's Yard are Lowes the butcher, and Crompton, Evans and Co., a rather exclusive bank that had gone by 1903. On the other side Jackson's was a chemist. The entrance to Sadler's Yard is still there. Above the ground floor the building is unchanged.

In Leeming Street it is the road surface that has undergone the most changes over the years. All the buildings visible in the 1906 photograph remain. The police box, just visible on the corner of the market, has disappeared. Traffic use is now restricted in favour of pedestrians.

For many years traffic was able to use the roads that ran around the market. Now access is restricted to market traders and stores. There has been very little change to the buildings that face the market.

The view from Albert Street towards the market shows little change apart from the alterations to the road and the disappearance of the tramway.

The Viaduct is prominent in both these photographs but there have been some minor changes. The shops beyond the viaduct have gone, to be replaced by an entrance to St Peter's Retail Park, which is landscaped with trees, and there are trees and seats in Market Street itself. You can just see the outline of Clerkson's Charity School behind the shops just beyond the Viaduct in the old photograph. At one time the Food Hall of the Co-op was on that site. Bird's, an old Mansfield firm, has moved to Leeming Street.

Offices and shops replaced the old property and garden at this end of Queen Street. The building adjacent to this once housed the Mechanics Institute.

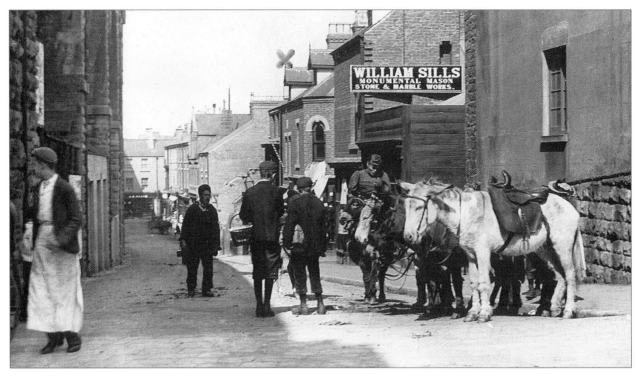

Shops and storehouses took advantage of the arches underneath the viaduct, as seen here in the 1900s. William Sills was a monumental mason. Most of the shop premises on the right are still there.

The Collins Building, erected by Mr Roe in 1910, replaced the Old White Bear.

The Hippodrome on Midworth Street opened in 1905 and became the Century in 1955. Unable to compete with other cinemas in the town it became a members-only bingo club in 1961. A new building replaced the old one, which was destroyed by fire in 1991, and it remains a popular bingo establishment.

In 2002 Lucas's garage remains and the Gala bingo hall dominates the scene, with the ring road slicing between them. The other former shops are now estate agents and offices.

Nottingham Road was a mainly residential area in 1912, with solid Victorian and Edwardian houses set in leafy gardens. The distinctive turreted building was the home of the cattle market keeper, built in 1877 to the design of Mansfield-born Watson Fothergill. The market opened for business on 1 January 1878 and closed in 1972.

The houses on Nottingham Road have seen little change over the years. Posters still adorn the corner of the property where Talbot Street meets the main road.

This part of Church Street is dominated by the arch of the railway viaduct. The archway of the Swan Hotel once allowed access for carriages. This entrance has now gone so the hotel can use the space for its guests.

The Swan was known as The Sign of the White Swan in early Tudor times and is probably the oldest hostelry in Mansfield. In the eighteenth and nineteenth centuries, the Swan was the foremost coaching centre in Mansfield and was the most luxurious inn for travellers needing accommodation. In 1910 modernisation began, with the introduction of electric power, the grassing-over of the old coach entrance to Swan Yard, and improvements to the rooms and plumbing. In 1936 the premises were brought up-to-date with the fitting out of a sherry bar, a residents' lounge panelled in oak and kitchens equipped with modern appliances and ovens. In 2002 the ground floor is open plan and the bar is a haunt of youthful drinkers.

This scene is still recognisable to those living in the twenty-first century, even though this photograph was taken in about 1915. Note the boy with his cart delivering goods; the magnificent gas street lamp; the tramlines with a tram in the distance; a soldier on horseback; and the adverts for snuff. Brittain's the jewellers was also an optician.

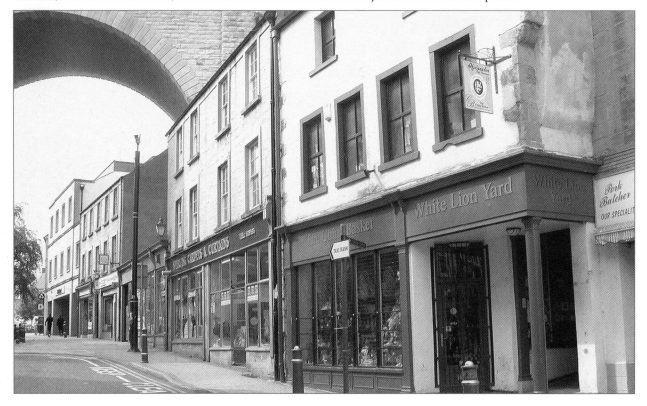

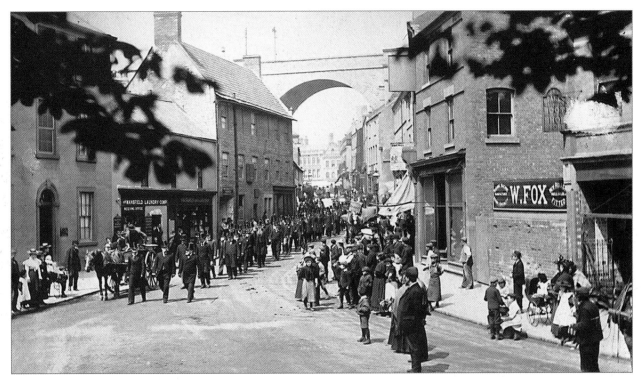

A mayoral procession to St Peter's. The new mayor would lead the town councillors to his chosen place of worship, where they dedicated themselves to serving the town. This was an important occasion and, as usual, quite a crowd turned out to watch the proceedings. The modern view is quite different. The school on the left has lost its lower aspect and has been turned into shops. The Eight Bells has been rebuilt and Fox's Bakery has gone.

The Ram Hotel on Church Street was
first recorded in 1732 and was probably
well established before then. The
building is certainly late medieval and
original timbers are visible in the
passage at the side of the inn. This was
one of Mansfield's ancient byways,
known as Maltkiln Court. The 'magpie'
effect on the façade was applied in the
1920s.

Skills' was originally a Tudor house but was demolished when the road was widened. On the other side of Toothill Lane is the handsome eighteenth-century building called Toothill House, at one time the Mansfield Trustees Saving Bank. When Shacklock's, solicitors, took over they restored the building to its previous appearance. At one time it was the vicarage to St Peter's Church.

Gilcroft Chambers, which was used by the council, lay in the path of the new ring road. Church Lane now continues under the ring road for pedestrians.

The place where Leeming Street begins to dip steeply towards the market place was identified as a potential accident black-spot in the days when car brakes were less reliable and drivers less experienced. The junction with Toothill Lane was one of the first in Mansfield to be marked, in 1904, with a 'caution board' and the presence of the policeman in this picture suggests traffic control measures. The Brunt's Charity Offices were built in 1918; the statue of local benefactor Samuel Brunt, who died in 1711, still occupies its niche overlooking a mock-Tudor estate agent's and several fast-food shops. The building on the corner is now Morley's dress shop.

The Stag & Pheasant and the Masons Arms have recently undergone extensive changes and extensions. With the Bowl in Hand a few yards further along, this part of Leeming Street is well served with public houses.

Clumber Street, formerly Back Lane West, viewed from its junction with Leeming Street. This area has undergone great change, with many new buildings. In the distance there used to be an amusement arcade but this has now been replaced by shops.

The approach to Leeming Street from Woodhouse Road has undergone dramatic changes, as these two views reveal. Although the buildings on the left remain, a whole terrace of houses has disappeared and the site is now dominated by the complex of traffic lights controlling entry to the bypass. In the background the lately disused ABC/Cannon cinema is now a snooker centre.

The ladies' hairdresser and grocery establishments on Leeming Street have now been merged together to house an insurance agent's business. Between 1965 and 1980 the grocer's shop, under new owners, was also a sub-post office. The proprietor, Sid Dearnley, had worked as a public executioner from 1949 to 1953.

The Yew Tree and the Eagle, side by side on Woodhouse Road, yielded to the bypass and road improvement schemes and disappeared in 1993. On the opposite side of the road the original Brunt's School buildings (not shown here) have been almost completely removed.

The view from Clumber Street towards the start of Chesterfield Road, now part of the inner ring road. A yard on the lower left-hand side housed a horse and cart that were used for street cleaning into the 1960s.

Beard & Freeman, agricultural merchants and seedsmen, occupied this site on Toothill Lane for many years. It had previously been used as the town pound. The main building behind the car park is the rear of the Bridge Street Methodist Chapel.

On the right is the original workhouse wall, and in both photographs you can just see the eighteenth-century Mansfield Union Workhouse. It became the Victoria Hospital and is now the Community Care Hospital. The road was widened very considerably. The public house, William IV, remains.

Cromwell House, the dominant building in both these pictures, is one of the oldest properties in the town. Though much restored, it may have been built in the sixteenth century. Towards the end of the eighteenth century it was the home of the Revd Samuel Catlow, the minister of the Old Meeting House. In one of its many rooms he operated a private academy, offering a superior education for boys aspiring to professional or commercial careers. The white-fronted building next to Cromwell House was demolished in the 1980s to make way for the inner ring road.

When it was built in 1754 Waverley House would have been the home of one of the town's most well-to-do citizens. Today it is one of Mansfield's oldest buildings and appears to be in a better condition than it was a hundred years ago when it was the premises of Mr C. Scott, a painter and decorator. The market cross in front of it was, in days gone by, a focal point in the life of the town. Official notices were read from its steps. In 1788 John Adams of Nottingham conducted an outdoor service from the cross which led to the formation of the first Methodist church in the town.

West Gate, from Waverley House to the Granada cinema. Gone now are the modest-fronted shops and houses of earlier times and in their place is the featureless block of the Four Seasons Shopping Centre, its bleakness partly concealed by a few trees. Built between 1973 and 1974, it also houses a large public library on the upper floor. The queen officially opened the new library on her visit to the town in 1977.

The rather run-down public house bearing the name of Nottingham brewers Shipstone was actually called the Nag's Head, once a popular hostelry but since closed. Sensitively rebuilt, it is now a shop, although it still displays signs of its previous life. The two statuettes of horses' heads that used to adorn the front of the inn have been retained as a reminder of bygone Mansfield. A monthly farmers' market is held around the old Butter Cross in West Gate, where fresh, local produce is available.

Construction of the Four Seasons Shopping Centre began after a great number of properties had been demolished. This did not interfere with the market stall-holders on West Gate. *Below*: Demolition moves forward towards the Granada cinema, where it would finally stop on this part of West Gate. Poyser's jewellers, in the centre-left of this photograph, is now a baker's shop.

Transport

A goods railway, horse-drawn, connected the town to the canal system at Pinxton in 1819. By the middle of the century it was steam-powered for both goods and passenger traffic. Passenger traffic was axed by the Beeching Act but was reinstated in the 1990s with the introduction of the Robin Hood Line. Road traffic in 1900 was principally horse-drawn. Individuals used cycles, many of which were produced locally. On 30 June 1898 the 'Pioneer' steam omnibus arrived in the town but lasted only two months because of technical problems. The opening of the Electricity Works on 17 June 1903 was followed in 1905 by the formation of the Mansfield Light Railway Company's tramway system which ran until 1932. By 1917 motor cycles were popular, and cars became more common in the 1920s. By 1926 the motor omnibus had arrived and remains today as the major form of public transport. This photograph was taken during work on the railway bridge close to Hermitage Mill.

The Midland Railway station was built in 1872 in an Italianate style when the branch line to Nottingham was extended to Worksop. When passenger traffic ceased in 1964 the station fell out of use and was for a time used as a night-club. It has recently been restored for the Robin Hood Line, which serves Nottingham and Worksop.

Locomotive no. 44658 passing through the railway station. Note the canopies over the platforms that gave shelter to passengers – but also covered them with smuts and made the station dark and gloomy.

After closure the platforms were removed. When passenger services resumed in November 1995 new platforms were built with simple shelters.

The original steep footpath up to the station has been replaced with steps.

The Mansfield branch of the Great Central Railway opened in 1917. The station was on Great Central Road and is seen here from the Newgate Lane crossroads. The railway station has gone and the embankment has been removed. The new police station now occupies the site of the old railway station.

The bridge on the corner of Baums Lane and Littleworth served the Great Central line. When it was demolished much of the land beyond was purchased by the Mansfield Brewery Company for expansion.

Two railway bridges crossed the Nottingham Road on either side of Baums Lane. They and their embankments have since been removed. On the left were some motor dealers which have now been replaced by a pizza restaurant, a fitness centre, motor accessory factors and a DIY store.

The Thompson family of Stanton Hill started in business with a horse-drawn cab service. They progressed to motorised transport and were involved with the start of the Mansfield Traction Co.

Mansfield's first steam-powered fire engine arrived in 1900. The more modern engines shown below date from 1984.

The corner of Stockwell Gate and Bancroft Lane, 1917. Chapman's cycle shop illustrates how important the bicycle was to the townspeople at this period. The building in the background is the Red Lion, now a restaurant and fitness centre.

Nottingham Road near Green Lane has changed very little over the years.

Chesterfield Road, *c.* 1905. At this time it marked the boundary between town and countryside. Buildings were few, trees abounded and, as the picture shows, traffic was both slow and light. Signs of change were apparent though. It is just possible to see the recently laid tram lines, along which, from 1905, townspeople could travel to Pleasley for one old penny. The tram service closed in 1932. The road is now much wider although there are still plenty of trees. Traffic is usually much heavier than is shown, too.

Social, Civic &
Recreational Life

Urban development requires the control of many aspects of social behaviour and the provision of amenities of many kinds. Some are essential, while others help to enhance the quality of life. One amenity which met with great enthusiasm was the introduction of the cinema. At one time Mansfield had six purpose-built cinemas, some proving more popular than others. The town now has just the one multiplex cinema which opened at the end of 1997.

The white stone Court House seen above was added in 1932 to the existing police station and Court House of 1873 (now demolished). The new Court House on Rosemary Street was officially opened by the Princess Royal on 8 July 1996.

The old police station, built in 1873 at the junction of Station Street and Commercial Street. To the rear were later additions. It has recently been demolished to make way for the St Peter's Retail Park. The new police station has its main entrance on Great Central Road, on the site of the former Great Central Railway station.

The 1873 police court at the junction of Station Street and Commercial Street (handily placed for transporting prisoners by rail to Bagthorpe Prison in Nottingham) was described as 'one of the handsomest buildings the town possesses', but, unsurprisingly perhaps, it never commanded the affection of Mansfield residents. When it was demolished in 2001 the stone was used in this façade overlooking Albert Street at the entrance to the new St Peter's Retail Park.

Mansfield's first fire station was built on Toothill Lane in 1815 and was rebuilt on the same site later in the nineteenth century. Although there were proposals to build a larger station on Ratcliffe Gate in the 1920s, the old building remained in use until 1939. The Toothill Lane site was cleared in 1970.

In 1939 a new fire station complex was opened on Rosemary Street, with adjacent houses for firemen. This complex was replaced by a new building in 1997, but the training tower still stands.

SOCIAL, CIVIC & RECREATIONAL LIFE

The original indoor public baths of 1853. Later expansion to the right of this building gave it a larger main pool. This was all demolished to make way for the Water Meadows leisure centre in 1990. The picture below shows the entrance to the new complex.

The main pool in the old swimming baths had cubicles close to the pool sides. This has all been replaced by the Water Meadows leisure centre which is able to meet the needs of both serious swimmers and youngsters with a choice of different pools and facilities.

Nearly a century separates these views of the bowling green in Westfield Lane Recreation Ground, but the pavilion is practically unchanged. The 2002 photograph shows a greatly improved green, but there are fewer spectators and no flower-beds. Evidently, bowling is not so much a spectator sport these days.

The Picturedrome on Belvedere Street dates from 1920. It has had a mixed history, serving at various times as a cinema, billiards hall, variety theatre, restaurant and offices for local government departments. More recently it has been used as a dance school, a private social club and a night-club. The street outside the building has now been lowered as part of the many road improvements in the town.

The Princes' Rink on Church Lane was purpose-built for roller-skating. Opened on 23 December 1909, it was initially popular but was forced to close on 22 April 1911. It was then redecorated and opened in October 1911 as the YMCA Hall. Since then it has been used for a variety of purposes.

The fields of Cumberlands Farm in the severe winter of 1946/7. The Lady Brook is in the foreground. This area would become part of Mansfield's first postwar council estate. The Lady Brook was piped underground but still occasionally welled up and flooded parts of the town during periods of heavy rain. Both photographs were taken from the same place on Brick Kiln Lane.

The urgent need for housing after the Second World War was met by the construction of prefabricated bungalows. This was the first one to be erected in Mansfield, on the Goodacre estate off Pelham Street. It was intended for a family of four, and the furniture was supplied by Mr W.A. Symington of the Co-operative Central Stores. Although originally designed to have only a limited life, many pre-fabs were subsequently clad in traditional building materials and some are still in use half a century later.

Albert Street was originally known as the Cockpit, since the town's cockfighting pit stood at the rear of the Cock Inn. Later this became the Top White Bear (there was a Bottom White Bear just a few hundred yards away) and finally, after 1887, The Victoria Hotel. The older picture was taken about 1920. The inn was rebuilt and enlarged in 1925.

The Festival Gardens were opened in 1954 to celebrate the 1951 Festival of Britain. The gardens were laid out on the 1763 extension to St Peter's burial ground, long disused and neglected. The old headstones were laid down to form paths and a rose and clematis pergola was erected. This pleasant oasis was cleared away sixteen years later, when the inner ring road was under construction.

Queen Elizabeth, consort of King George VI, visited Mansfield in 1948 and went on to lay the foundation stone of Portland Training College. A year later Princess Elizabeth and the Duke of Edinburgh came to open the college.

Queen Elizabeth II leaving Queen Elizabeth's School after officially opening the new additions to the school in March 1997.

94

Industry

Rock Valley, *c.* 1925. Mansfield's industry can be divided into four main categories, all shaped by the town's location. These are quarrying and mining, processing crops grown locally, processing animals and engineering. There are other subsidiary industries. Water from the River Maun was an early source of power. Later on sand was quarried, for brick-making and foundry work, thus encouraging the development of engineering firms. The main local crop was barley, which formed the basis of the malting and brewing industry. In the mid-nineteenth century there were about forty maltings in the town and later the well-known brewery was founded. At the end of the eighteenth century there was much unemployment in the town and the Duke of Portland instigated the building of six spinning mills to provide work for Mansfield's men. Most of these mills still stand today (though now put to other uses). When spinning declined frameworking started up for stockings and lace. Hosiery working carried on into the twentieth century. The machines needed servicing and the skilled mechanics who maintained them formed another strand in the development of engineering. Coal mining reached the area in 1875–6 when Pleasley Pit was sunk by the Stanton Ironworks Company. The next adjacent pit was Sherwood colliery, sunk at Mansfield Woodhouse in 1902. Mansfield colliery at Crown Farm was sunk by the Bolsover Colliery Company in 1904–6 with production starting in 1906 from the Top Hard seam.

In 1800 William Brodhurst was described as probably 'the largest maltster in England'. At this time there were as many as forty maltings in the town. The maltings on Midworth Street, formerly Blind Lane, was built by Brodhurst in about 1787. In the 1980s it was converted into a night-club.

Windsor Road was known as Kate Moody's Lane when this photograph was taken in about 1900. On the left is Abraham's mill, one of many examples of industry in Mansfield. The house to the right is Rock Lodge, which was the home of the Abraham family (and remained so until comparatively recently). The derelict Jackson's mill can be seen in the distance. In 2002 no trace of the mills can be seen. The fields in which they stood were quarried by the Abrahams for the valuable moulding sand which underlies the southern part of Mansfield. Rock Lodge is still a residence and the former quarry is now Fisher Lane Recreation Ground.

Club Mill, also known as Rock Mill and later Jackson's Mill, stood near the junction of Carter Lane and Southwell Road. It was rebuilt as a tower mill in 1821 with four sails and four storeys. Disused by 1900, it was pulled down in about 1905. The picture dates from 1895. The view today is very different.

Mansfield Brewery was founded in 1855 on its current site in Littleworth. In the last half of the twentieth century the company grew rapidly, developing a large base in the East Midlands. The purchase of the Hull Brewery extended its influence into South Yorkshire and made it one of the largest independent brewers in the country. By 1994 it employed about 4,000 people and owned over 5,400 public houses. It was purchased by the Wolverhampton & Dudley Brewery at the end of 1999. Production of Mansfield beers was transferred to Park Brewery, Wolverhampton, in December 2001 when the Mansfield Brewery closed. Part of the buildings is now the Making It museum.

In 1785 William Smith converted an old corn mill into a cotton spinning mill. Field Mill was one of seven water-powered spinning mills built between 1790 and 1800 along the River Maun between Little Matlock Mill and Bath Mill. It had the largest waterwheel in the town. For most of the nineteenth century it was occupied by Messrs Greenhalgh. Other manufacturing activities were also carried out, including leather-working. The mill was virtually derelict by 1900; the wheel was removed in the early 1920s and the building was demolished in 1925. The Master's House remains as a public house.

The Ellis Brothers, early nineteenth-century Quakers, opened a mustard mill in Rock Valley. It was taken over in 1839 by David Cooper Barringer. In 1873 it was decided to produce decorative metal mustard boxes and these became so popular that a new factory was built in 1889 to concentrate on making them. In December 1895 it became Barringer, Wallis & Manners' tin factory, with 143 employees. In 1939 it was incorporated into the Metal Box Company. The first picture shows the factory before the ring road was built.

Portland Cotton Mill was founded by Mary Cash and her family in about 1839. It was the first steam-powered mill in the town. Whiteley Radio moved there in 1932. The later picture shows how little change there has been over the years. The works chimney to the left has gone and a new building has been inserted but otherwise these two views are very similar.

Mansfield Colliery at Crown Farm, 1920. It was sunk in 1904–6 by the Bolsover Colliery Company. The managing director was John Plowright Houfton who was very active locally and even built 'model villages' for his workforce. He became Mayor of Mansfield and MP for East Nottingham, and was knighted in 1928. He died in 1929. The Bolsover Company also owned Rufford, Clipstone and Thorseby pits and was the third largest colliery company in the country. Crown Farm Industrial Park has now replaced the pit.

Sherwood Colliery was sunk in 1902–3 by the Ellis family, who had earlier opened collieries in Hucknall. They ran the pit until nationalisation in 1947. In 1989 it produced a million tons of coal and employed eight hundred men. It was closed in January 1992 and demolished.

John Harwood Cash established Lawn Mills in Rosemary Street in 1907. In 1973 the firm was taken over by Courtaulds, with a turnover of some £15 million and a thousand employees. The takeover was not successful and the factory closed. It was subsequently converted into the Rosemary Centre complex of offices and shops which opened in 1984.

These shops, now demolished, stood at the bottom of Sutton Road. A & C Sports Ltd was a bicycle shop. Behind it is the Shoe Company. In 1871 George Appelbee Royce was in partnership here with John James Gascoine making riveted boots. It became a limited company in 1876 and in 1900 became Mansfield Shoe Co. Ltd of Dallas Street. In 1935 it was a founder member of the Norvic Group and in the 1960s and 1970s had seven hundred employees. Norvic went into receivership in 1981 but the Mansfield Shoe Co. (1981) Ltd survives. Its turnover in 1991 was £14,550,000.

Boneham & Turner, precision engineers, was founded in 1918 in a workshop at Field Mill but moved to the Duke Street Works in Portland Street in 1922. The above photograph shows John Boneham and staff outside the Duke Street Works in 1930. This site has now disappeared under the ring road. Below is the Nottingham Road factory, built in three stages, the first being completed in 1936.

This building on Sherwood Street was once the
hosiery factory of Alcock & Co. Used by a number of
other firms in the 1970s, it has since been removed
and the site has recently been redeveloped.

The Town Mill had many more storeys until a fire in 1907. Originally a cotton mill, it has now been converted into a public house.

Sherwood Foundry was established in 1788 by Luke Abbott. James Maude arrived on the scene in 1840. Among other things the firm made post-boxes (marked Colin Ching and W.T. Allen) and dolphin lampposts for the Embankment in London. The works are seen here in about 1940, when the workmen's cottages were unoccupied. The outer wall of the cottage gardens was retained after the expansion of the works.

The council joinery department building used to stand on Toothill Lane, but has now been demolished. The empty site is now used as a car park.

Church & Education

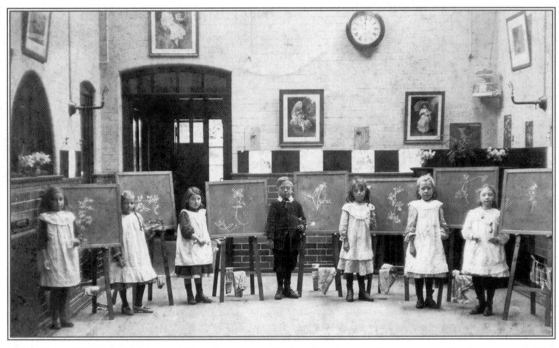

Before the 1870 Education Act the Church was strongly linked with education as most schools were created by bequests to the Church for the education of boys (such as Queen Elizabeth's Grammar School for Boys) or were set up by charities for the education of poor children (such as Faith Clerkson and Thompson's). Well-off parents sent their children to private schools, such as Mr Maltby's Academy in Rock Court. Many Sunday Schools developed into day schools; the Bridge Street Wesleyan School, for example, had so many pupils that when King Edward's Council School was built on St Catherine's Street in Littleworth in 1903 it could happily supply the new school with sufficient pupils. Here we see children displaying their artistic efforts in King Edward's school hall, which is typical of the period. During the following century schools have gone through drastic changes, from elementary, secondary modern and grammar schools, to the comprehensive system comprising first, middle and upper schools, and then the more usual infant, junior and senior establishments.

This was one of the last pictures taken of the West Gate Congregational (United Reform) Church before its spire was removed. Designed by Mansfield-born Fothergill Watson, it opened for use in 1878. It was closed in 1981. The Round House surgery now occupies the site.

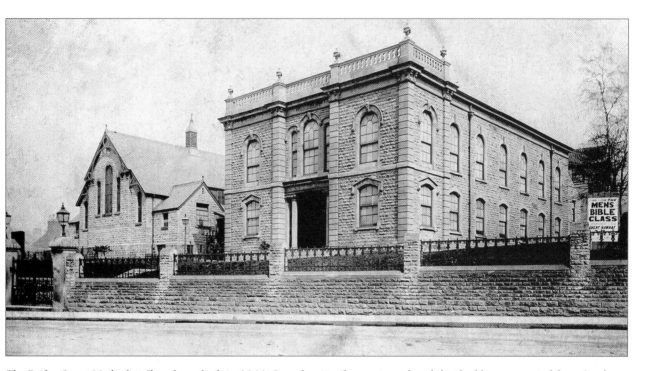

The Bridge Street Methodist Chapel was built in 1864–5 on the site of a previous chapel that had been converted from Stanhope House, a residence of the Earls of Chesterfield. In 1887 a large building was added to the site as a school for both day and Sunday pupils. In its heyday, in about 1900, the chapel was well supported, counting members of the borough council and other prominent families among its followers. There were about a thousand children on the books of its Sunday School.

St Lawrence's Church at the junction of Skerry Hill and Peck's Hill, viewed from Newgate Lane. The Wesleyan Reform Church on Bolsover Street is now used as St Lawrence's parish centre. Halfway up on the right, the Rock Cinema showed films until 1956. Its roof is just visible over the properties in the foreground.

The Rosemary Street Baptist Church was built in 1912 in a traditional style with galleries and a large choir. An organ was installed in 1920. On the extreme right of the picture is the Belle Vue public house and on the left is the Empire Theatre. Both would fall victim to road widening. Lawn Mills in the background (now the Rosemary Centre) has survived but all the other buildings have gone and a bus station occupies the site of the church.

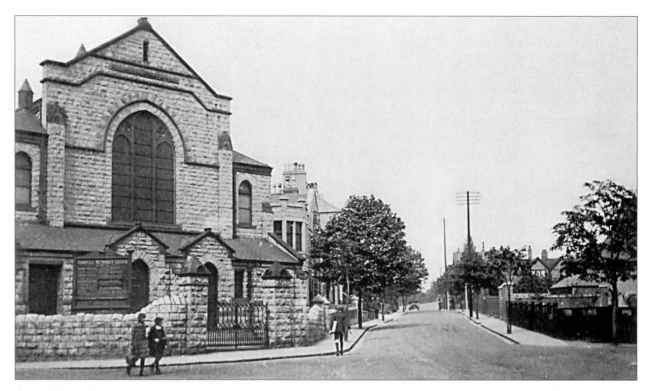

The Primitive Methodist Church on the corner of Woodhouse Road and Terrace Road dates from 1886–7. Closed in 1960, it is now used by a group of Christians in the Evangelical/Pentecostal tradition.

This building on St John's Street, formerly Catlow Street, dates from 1838. Originally a Wesleyan New Connection chapel, in 1870 it was sold and became a hosiery warehouse. It later housed the Stokes Castings Sports and Social Club (as shown here) and is now a bedding and furniture salesroom.

The Carnegie Library was built in 1905. In 1931 a new reference section was added in a second storey. It was superseded by the new library above the Four Seasons Shopping Centre and is now used as an arts centre.

The museum was brought into prominence in 1989 when the alley between the Palace Theatre complex and the former Carnegie Library was roofed over and an arched entrance erected on Leeming Street. This provided extra exhibition space and has been used to set out displays illustrating various aspects of the town's history. This extension was officially opened by Sarah, Duchess of York on 2 May 1989. (*See also* pp. 122–3).

This photograph was taken from the bottom of Blind Lane, renamed Midworth Street in 1913. The cottage was the residence of the assistant usher at the Grammar School, housed in the old building behind his house. In 1878 the school moved to new premises on Chesterfield Road and the cottage was pulled down in the course of widening this narrow and hazardous corner. The school building then became St Peter's National School and later a Church of England primary school. In 1974 St Peter's Primary School moved to new buildings on Bellamy Road and the old site then became the parish centre, which has been refurbished and expanded.

On the opposite corner of Station Street was the Faith Clerkson's Charity School building. It ceased to be a school in 1900 but scholarships for further education continued until the 1930s. This view dates from 1972 but by 1986 all the buildings on the right of Station Street had gone. They have now been replaced by the St Peter's Retail Park development.

Mansfield Technical College was built in 1928 on Chesterfield Road. In 1930 the School of Art moved into the early nineteenth-century Ashfield House, which stands behind the college. The whole site now houses various departments of the West Nottinghamshire College, both in the original buildings and in the later additions.

W.E. Baily was a man of leisure. Born in Mansfield, he lived most of his life in Penzance where he indulged his hobby of collecting natural history specimens and other curiosities. He even had a corrugated iron shed built in which to display these objects. After his death it was discovered that he had bequeathed both the building and its contents to his home town. They were duly transported to Mansfield and on 6 July 1904 the mayoress, Mrs J.F. Alcock, opened the town's first museum.

For many years the museum suffered because it was out of sight of passers-by on Leeming Street. Set back from the road at the end of a narrow alley, it remained virtually hidden even though the entrance to the permanent building of 1938 was quite impressive.

Mr William Daws was the original museum's
first curator, moving with the building and its
contents from Cornwall to Mansfield. He served
as curator until his retirement in 1928, when
he was succeeded by his grandson who
continued the family tradition until 1973.

The new museum, which opened in 1938, had a more imposing entrance. As well as providing more exhibition space, the
new building also included a combined lecture hall and art gallery. On permanent display are natural history specimens from
the Joseph Whitaker collection, a fine display of watercolours depicting bygone Mansfield by Albert Sorby Buxton, and pieces
of porcelain decorated by William Billingsley, some of which were made in Mansfield. Frequent temporary exhibitions make
regular visits worthwhile experiences.

First World War armistice celebrations in the Rosemary Street Elementary School playground. Opened in 1900 and closed 1977, the school was demolished in 2002. It was designed by the borough architect, R. Frank Vallance.

The Baptist Church and houses opposite the school were replaced by the bus station. The road between them, Rooth Street, ended at the high walls enclosing the grounds of the Old Meeting House. The school was demolished in 2002.

Acknowledgements

The Old Mansfield Society wishes to acknowledge its indebtedness to a number of people, in particular the staff of Mansfield Library, Mansfield Museum and the Editor of the *Mansfield Chronicle Advertiser*. Most of the illustrations in this book come from the archives of the Society. Our greatest debt is to John Vanags, who has been responsible for most of the modern photographs, for his help in compiling this book.

The Old Mansfield Society was formed in 1919 and is the second oldest Local History Society in Nottinghamshire. The Society's aims are to preserve records, artefacts and pictorial evidence of Mansfield and to allow both Society members and the wider public access to them. The society's website is www.old-mansfield.org.uk.

St Peter's Church.